PEGASUS ENCYCLOPEDIA LIBRARY

Experiments and Activities
BIOLOGY

Edited by: Aparna Chatterji
Managing editor: Tapasi De
Designed by: Vijesh Chahal and Anil Kumar
Illustrated by: Suman S. Roy, Tanoy Choudhury
Colouring done by: Vinay Kumar, Sonu, Kiran Kumari & Pradeep Kumar

CONTENTS

Introduction 3
How strong is an egg? 4
Which leaf preserves water? 5
Do plants drink water? 6
Making eyeglasses with fingers 8
Zigzag roots 9
The frightened earthworm 10
Self-watering flowers 11
Are you moving? 12
Do plants release water? 13
Are you stronger than air? 15
Measuring force 16
Which is quicker, gravity or the eye? 17
Lifting a water cup with the palm 18
Finding your blind spot 19
Potatoes with bird feathers 20
The lazy eye 21
Growing bread mould 22
Water with microscopic creatures 23
Flowers without stems 24
Floating lemon 25
Taste and smell go together 26
Sunlight and plants 27
How yeast breathes 28
Make your own greenhouse 29
Cells of an onion 30
How much air can your lungs hold? 31
Index 32

Introduction

Learning and experiencing new things is a continuous process. Children are much more inquisitive than we elders are. They are always bubbling with enthusiasm when it comes to knowing new things. That is the reason they are so full of questions. This enthusiasm should never be curbed; instead, it should be encouraged!

It is a proven fact that children learn the most by doing, experiencing and seeing things. Teaching them through books and worksheets only, does not suffice. We all know that 'seeing is believing'.

But sometimes due to the constraint of time and many other factors, elders are not successful in giving those experiences and exposure to their children which they deserve.

As a subject, Biology is important because it is the 'study of life'. It is the branch of science that tells us about plants, animals and human beings. This encyclopedia on Biology is full of interesting activities and experiments that will help the young readers to enhance their knowledge about the living things around them!

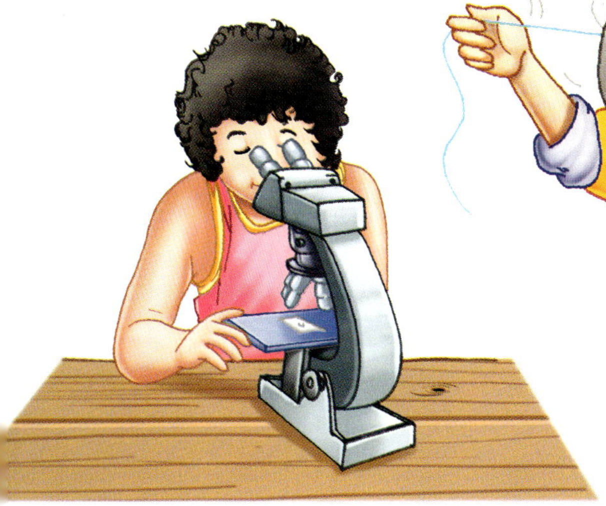

How strong is an egg?

The fact

We know that an egg is not hard to break because its shell isn't very strong. But an egg is perhaps not that fragile as it remains intact when it hits the ground when the hen lays it. Nature has taken care that an egg is both light and strong. Perform this experiment to check this out.

How to do the experiment?

1. Set the egg upright with the help of some clay on one side of the tray.
2. Put two piles of coins equaling the height of the egg on two opposite corners of the tray.
3. Place one book in the plastic bag in order to protect it and then balance it carefully on the egg and the coins.
4. Watch the egg carefully and place books on it, one by one. See how many can it hold before it breaks?

What you need

- A large tray
- An egg
- Clay
- A pile of coins
- A plastic bag
- Books

Conclusion

An egg is shaped like an arch at both ends. This is an excellent shape for bearing loads. Its strength along its axis is great because high arches spread loads. An egg is much easier to break on its sides because at the shallower arches they are weaker.

Introduction

Learning and experiencing new things is a continuous process. Children are much more inquisitive than we elders are. They are always bubbling with enthusiasm when it comes to knowing new things. That is the reason they are so full of questions. This enthusiasm should never be curbed; instead, it should be encouraged!

It is a proven fact that children learn the most by doing, experiencing and seeing things. Teaching them through books and worksheets only, does not suffice. We all know that 'seeing is believing'.

But sometimes due to the constraint of time and many other factors, elders are not successful in giving those experiences and exposure to their children which they deserve.

As a subject, Biology is important because it is the 'study of life'. It is the branch of science that tells us about plants, animals and human beings. This encyclopedia on Biology is full of interesting activities and experiments that will help the young readers to enhance their knowledge about the living things around them!

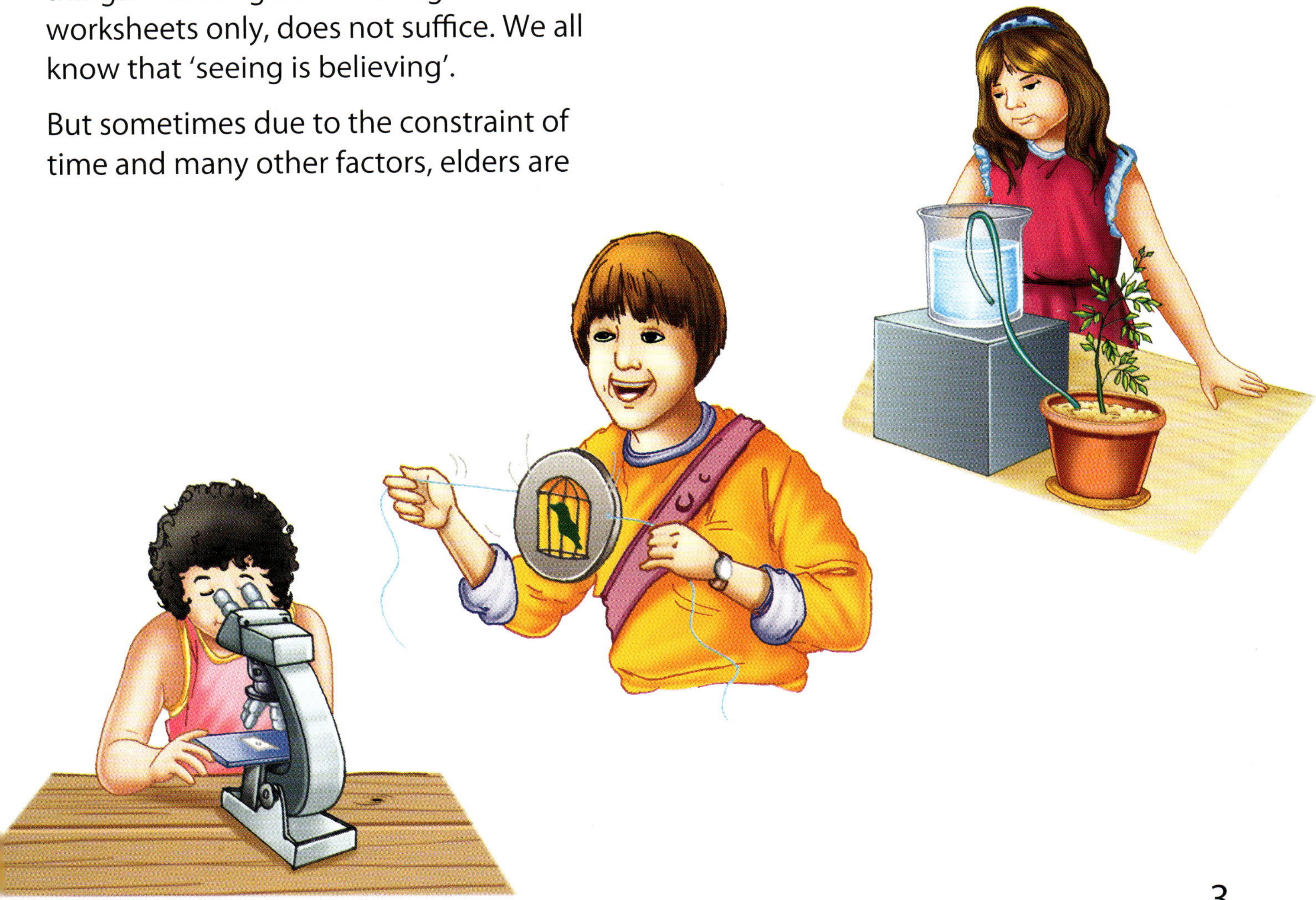

How strong is an egg?

The fact

We know that an egg is not hard to break because its shell isn't very strong. But an egg is perhaps not that fragile as it remains intact when it hits the ground when the hen lays it. Nature has taken care that an egg is both light and strong. Perform this experiment to check this out.

How to do the experiment?

1. Set the egg upright with the help of some clay on one side of the tray.
2. Put two piles of coins equaling the height of the egg on two opposite corners of the tray.
3. Place one book in the plastic bag in order to protect it and then balance it carefully on the egg and the coins.
4. Watch the egg carefully and place books on it, one by one. See how many can it hold before it breaks?

What you need

- A large tray
- An egg
- Clay
- A pile of coins
- A plastic bag
- Books

Conclusion

An egg is shaped like an arch at both ends. This is an excellent shape for bearing loads. Its strength along its axis is great because high arches spread loads. An egg is much easier to break on its sides because at the shallower arches they are weaker.

Which leaf preserves water?

The fact

Summers are often very dry. Leaves of many plants have certain structures or shapes which help them conserve moisture. Look for those which are able to retain water for the longest time.

What you need

- Cotton thread
- Different kinds of leaves
- Two tall sticks

How to do the experiment?

1. In a warm area, affix the two sticks on the ground leaving a little distance between them.
2. Tie the cotton thread between the two sticks.
3. Tie the leaves onto the thread.
4. Check the leaves every hour and note the changes observed.

Conclusion

Some leaves become very dry but some surprisingly do not look that dry. This means that these leaves have the capacity to hold back the moisture more than the others. These leaves usually have a waxy cuticle to prevent water loss. Some leaves also have curled up shapes which reduce the surface area to volume ratio, thereby decreasing water loss due to transpiration.

BIOLOGY

Do plants drink water?

The fact

We all know that water reaches plants from the soil through the roots and moves up through the stem. This experiment will show you how.

How to do the experiment?

1. Trim 1 cm off the bottom of your carnation stem and place it in the coloured water.
2. Keep it there for a few hours.

What will happen?

After sometime, the flowers will show traces of the colour of the water.

What you need

- White flowers (eg. Carnations or roses) with long stems
- Water coloured with ink or food dye
- A knife

Conclusion

The stalk of flowers contains tiny tubes called capillaries. When immersed in water, the molecules of the capillary walls which are in contact with water attract the water molecules which are the closest to them and raise them above the level of the water in the vessel. To this capillary phenomenon is added the osmotic pressure which takes the water all the way to the top of the flower.

Do plants drink water?

A step further

You may also do this experiment using various food colours and see which gives the best results.

The previous experiment can be taken a step further. Read the experiment given below and see how.

What you need

- A white flower (carnation, rose, dahlia)
- Two glasses of water
- Blue and red coloured dyes

How to do the experiment?

1. Colour the water in the two glasses— one red and one blue. To get brightly coloured flowers, add more colour to the water.
2. Ask an adult to carefully slit the stalk of the flower from the middle and lower the two halves into the two glasses standing side by side.
3. Wait for a few hours.

What will happen?

One half of the flower will have traces of blue and the other half traces of the red colour!

Conclusion

The stem or the stalk of the flower contains tiny tubes or capillaries called xylem, which carry the coloured water from the two glasses to the flower. Since the two halves of the stalk are placed in different coloured water, the flower gets coloured in different hues.

Making eyeglasses with fingers

Here is an activity that can only be performed by people those who are short-sighted.

How to perform the activity?

1. Bend your index finger and thumb to form a small opening as shown.
2. Look through the hole. Distant objects will appear sharper.

What happens?

The air in the hole acts as a convex lens which corrects short sightedness by directing the image towards the central yellow spot in your eye called the macula.

> **Yellow spot** or **macula** is an oval spot near the centre of the retina of the human eye. It has a size of 1.5 mm and it is specialized for seeing things with the highest clarity.

Zigzag roots

The fact

We know that the roots of plants always grow vertically downwards. Through this experiment let's turn some soil with seeds planted in it in different directions and see if we can 'confuse' the seeds!

What you need

- Germinated seeds (seedlings)
- Two sheets of blotting paper
- Two pieces of glass
- Two rubber bands
- A shallow vessel with some water

How to do the experiment?

1. Take the shoots and place them between the two sheets of blotting paper.
2. Place the blotting paper with the seedlings between the pieces of glass and seal them with the rubber bands as shown.
3. Place the glass in the vessel with water and put it near a window.
4. Every other day, flip the glass over to the opposite edge.

What will happen?

The roots will always grow downwards while the shoot will grow upwards, irrespective of the orientation of the glass.

Conclusion

Plants 'know' the direction of the Earth's core. The Earth's gravity always makes roots grow downwards. This phenomenon is called geotropism. The plant's shoot grows in the opposite direction. If you look at plants growing on hillsides, you will see that they always grow vertically.

The frightened earthworm

Here is a harmless activity involving an earthworm.

What you need

- A copper plate and a zinc plate (both rectangle shaped)
- A strip of sandpaper
- Some water

How to do the activity?

1. Clean the plates with sandpaper and wet them with water.
2. Place them on top of each other forming a cross and put the worm on one.

What will happen?

When the worm tries to cross over from one plate to the other, it is driven back.

Conclusion

When the copper and the zinc plates are brought in contact with water, certain chemical reactions take place across their surfaces. As a result of these reactions, when the earthworm touches both the metal plates at the same time, a weak current flows through its body and it is unable to proceed ahead.

Self-watering flowers

The fact

According to the principles of hydrodynamics, a liquid will flow from a container kept at a higher elevation to a lower elevation, if connected with a tube. This is due to a difference in the potential energy of the liquids kept at different elevations. This principle can be used to water your flower pots when you are away!

What you need

- A vessel to keep water
- A base for it (e.g. a box or a high carton)
- A thin rubber or plastic tube
- A flower pot

How to do the experiment?

1. Fill the vessel with water and place it on the base. This will increase the elevation of the water vessel with respect to the flower pot kept on the floor.

2. Dip one end of the thin tube into the water vessel and put the other into the flower pot.

What will happen?

The flower pot will always have a sufficient supply of water due to the principle of siphon.

Note: When you want the watering to begin, draw the air out from the end of the tube which is going into the flower pot. The water will begin to flow towards the pot, though at a slow rate because of the reduced atmospheric pressure acting on the end implanted into the earth. Another factor which causes the siphon to work is the difference in potential of the liquids kept at the different elevations. The difference in potential is caused due to gravity.

Conclusion

Both pressure and gravity play a part in the flow of fluids. The difference in pressure at each end pushes the water into the tube. Gravity pulls the fluid downward. If the effect of the pressure works with gravity, the fluid will flow. If it works against gravity, the fluid may not flow.

Are you moving?

The fact

When we are unable to see our surroundings, it is difficult to observe the change in our position relative to other things. So, it is difficult to understand whether we are moving or not. This experiment will help you understand this phenomenon.

What will happen?

The blindfolded person will never know whether she/he is moving or not!

What you need

A blindfold

How to perform the activity?

1. One of you should be blindfolded.
2. Then two others should carry that person as shown.
3. The children who are the bearers should alternate forward steps with stepping up and down while standing still.

Conclusion

When we are unable to see our surroundings, we cannot observe the change in our position relative to other things. We will therefore not be sure if we are moving or not.

Do plants release water?

The fact

Plants absorb water from the soil. Some of this water is released into the atmosphere as water vapour by the process called transpiration.

What you need?

- A potted plant
- Plastic bag
- Adhesive tape

How to do the experiment?

1. Cover the plant with the plastic bag.
2. Using the tape, seal the bag around the stem taking care not to damage the plant.
3. Wait for a day.

What will happen?

You will observe tiny droplets on the inner surface of the bag.

Conclusion

Plants release some water through tiny pores in their leaves called stomata.

A step further

You may do another experiment in a totally different manner having the same outcome.

What you need

A large plastic jar with a wide opening

Some nutrient rich humus

Charcoal and gravel

Small plants like ivy

Ferns and mosses

About 250 mm of water

How to do the experiment?

1. Spread the gravel at the bottom of the jar. Place a layer of charcoal on top of it.
2. Put a layer of soil about 10 cm thick on the charcoal.
3. Carefully take selected plants from their pots and plant them in the jar.
4. Water the soil but make sure it isn't too wet.
5. Put the lid on the jar and place it in a warm and well-lit spot, but not in direct sunlight.

What will happen?

Tiny droplets of water will be seen on the walls of the jar.

Conclusion

Plants do give out some water out of what they have consumed.

Are you stronger than air?

The fact

Although, we are generally quite unaware of its existence, air pressure affects us all the time. Let us see this through this simple activity.

What you need

Two bathroom rubber suction cups

How to do the experiment?

1. Hold the cups together as shown and force some air out of them.
2. After sometime, try and pull them apart. You will see that it isn't as easy as it appears.

Conclusion

Placing the cups together forms a sphere. When you expel some of the air inside them, you actually help in reducing the pressure inside. The outside air pressure is then enough to hold them together tightly.

Measuring force

The fact

Force is defined as an influence that tends to cause an object to undergo a change in speed, direction or shape. We cannot see force itself, but we can see its effect. In order to move an object from a state of rest or to be stopped, a force must be exerted on it.

All people exert force by using the strength of their muscles. If you have a dynamometer or a spring scale, you can measure your own muscle strength in the following way.

What you need

- A spring scale
- A bottle and a cork stopper
- A corkscrew
- A piece of cord

Note: The dynamometer works on the principle of an elastic spring – the stronger the force, the more the spring is extended and further it moves the pointer.

How to do the activity?

1. Loop one end of the cord around your foot and attach the other to the dynamometer.
2. Pull the dynamometer upwards.

What will happen?

The pointer on the dynamometer will move and show the force which you are exerting.

A step further

You can also measure the force needed to extract a cork from a bottle, with the use of the dynamometer.

Which is quicker, gravity or the eye?

The fact

Gravity is a mysterious force. Everyone knows that it exists yet it is very difficult to understand it. It is gravity that is responsible for the planet Earth attracting all other objects. When you see images of astronauts seemingly floating in space in a state of complete weightlessness that does not mean that the Earth is not exerting a gravitational force on them. Here is a way to use the force of gravity for a game.

What you need

- White cardboard
- A ruler
- A pen and a pair of scissors

How to perform the activity?

1. Cut out a piece of white cardboard 30 cm long and 5 cm wide.
2. Mark 5 cm divisions on the cardboard making six segments in all.
3. Ask a friend to hold the cardboard hanging vertically just above your hand.
4. When your friend drops the cardboard, try and catch it as quickly as you can.
5. What will happen?
6. However easy it looks, you will never be able to catch the bottom end of the cardboard.

A step further

Have your friend drop a ping pong ball down a tube held vertically. Try and smack the ball with a ruler as it leaves the tube and before it hits the ground.

Conclusion

This happens because it is a race between gravity and your body. By the time the message from your brain reaches the muscles of your hand, gravity pulls the cardboard down several centimetres.

Lifting a water cup with the palm

What you need

A plastic cup full of water

How to perform the activity?

1. Place the cup full of water on the table.
2. Moisten the palm of your hand and press it down flat on the cup, bending your fingers as shown.
3. Now straighten your fingers, but continue to press down on the cup.
4. Now lift your hand slowly.

What will happen?

The cup will stay attached to the palm of your hand.

Conclusion

By pressing down on the cup you expel a little air. This makes the outside air pressure stronger than that of the rarified air inside and that it what holds the cup attached to your hand.

Finding your blind spot

What you need

A piece of cardboard inscribed as shown below with a cross and a dot.

How to do the activity?

1. Hold the strip exactly 38 cm from your eyes, close your left eye and focus the other eye on the 'X' written on the cardboard.
2. Slowly move the strip closer until first the square and then the dot disappears.
3. Keep moving the strip closer until the square and the dot appear again.

The fact

The blind spot in the eye does not contain light-sensitive cells and does not respond to light. So the images that fall on it are not seen at all.

What will happen?

When the image of the square falls on the blind spot it won't be seen. The same happens with the black spot.

Conclusion

The Blind Spot does not contain light-sensitive cells and does not respond to light. In other words, it cannot transform light into nerve impulses as it happens in the Yellow Spot (the sensitive region of the eye's retina).

Potatoes with bird feathers

The fact

This experiment will show the effect of bird feathers as they fly through the air.

What you need

- A small potato
- Six to eight bird feathers

How to do the experiment?

1. Drop the potato and note its flight through the air.
2. Now stick the feathers into the potato as shown in the picture and drop it from the same height.

What will happen?

The potato drops more slowly and rotates as it falls.

The feathers provide strong air resistance, while the featherless potato has an easier time forcing its way through the air.

A step further

Try and run with an open umbrella trailing behind you and then run without it. Which will be easier and why?

The lazy eye

The fact
Our eye retains an image for a fraction of a second after it has disappeared. This is due to the 'laziness' of the eye.

What you need
- A piece of cardboard
- A pin
- Two pieces of string and a pencil

How to do the activity?
Cut out a circular piece of cardboard.

1. On one side draw an empty cage and on the other a bird (upside down).
2. Make two small holes with the pin on both the sides of the circular cardboard. Insert strings through them and fasten.
3. Rotate the strings a number of times and then pull them apart rotating the cardboard.

What will happen?
It will appear as if the bird is inside the cage!

Conclusion
What happens is the effect caused by the 'laziness' of the eye. This means that our eye retains an image for a fraction of a second even after it has disappeared. When the image of the cage appears, the image of the bird still lingers in our vision. The two images merge with each other forming a single image of a bird in a cage.

BIOLOGY

Growing bread mould

The fact

Perform this experiment to demonstrate that Bread Mold spores are present anywhere and everywhere.

What is a Bread Mold?

Bread Mold is a simple fungus which gets its food from a variety of materials like grains, fruits, vegetables or flesh. Mold spores are tiny and usually remain suspended in the air. As soon as it finds the right environment for it to grow, the spores transform into the living fungus.

What you need

- Piece of bread
- Re-sealable airtight plastic bag
- Dropper
- Cotton swab
- Milk carton
- Adhesive tape
- Water
- Disposable rubber hand gloves for protection

How to do the experiment?

1. Collect dust from the ground on a piece of cotton cloth.
2. Rub this soiled cloth on a slice of bread.
3. Put 5 or 6 drops of water on the bread slice.
4. Put this bread slice in an airtight bag and seal it.
5. Place this sealed bag in an empty milk carton (preferably with milk remains in it) and seal the carton.
6. Leave the set-up undisturbed for a day or two.

What will happen?

After two days, when the sealed package will be opened, the bread slice will be covered with Bread Mold of various colours and textures.

Conclusion

Spores develop into living fungus when it gets suitable conditions. The bread slice had adequate nutrition and moisture necessary for the Mold spores to germinate.

Water with microscopic creatures

The fact

Water is generally the home to many interesting creatures and microorganisms, especially if its dirty water. Take some samples, view them under a microscope and see what you can find.

What you need

- A concave slide
- A dropper
- A microscope
- Different samples of water (tap water, pond water, muddy water etc).

How to do the experiment?

1. Set up your microscope using its highest setting.
2. Use the dropper to take some water from one of your samples and put it on the concave slide. Focus the microscope properly and try to see the living organisms swimming in it.
3. After observing their movements you can record their behaviours and draw them too.

What are you looking at?

Some of the creatures and microorganisms you might be able to see include:

Euglenas: Any unicellular organism belonging to the genus Euglena that lives in freshwater, have a cylindrical or sausage-like shape and move by means of a whip-like flagellum.

Protozoa: Any of a large group of unicellular, usually microscopic, eukaryotic organisms, such as amoebas, ciliates, flagellates and sporozoans.

Amoebas: Amoebas are one-celled protozoa. These microorganisms swim by wobbling. They also surround their food like a blob in order to eat it.

Algae: These are not considered to be plants by most scientists; these organisms might be yellowish, greenish or reddish in colour.

There might be larger creatures such as worms or brine shrimp in your water samples depending on where you took them from.

Flowers without stems

The fact

We know that stems are a necessary part of a plant for its survival. This activity will help you understand this.

What do you need

- 2 fresh flowers
- Scissors
- Pencil or pen
- Journal

How to do the activity?

1. Cut the stem of one of the flowers using a pair of scissors.
2. Place both the flowers (one with the stem, one without a stem) in a safe place.
3. After an hour, check the plants and note any noticeable difference in your journal.
4. Now wait for 24 hours and check the plants again. Do not forget to take down the differences in your journal.
5. Repeat step 4 for 2 more days. Observe what happens to the plants.

What will happen?

The flower without the stem will wilt off much faster than the flower with the stem.

Conclusion

The stem of a flower holds water whether they are in a vase or in the ground. The stem draws up water to keep their petals moist and healthy. When the stem was cut off from one of the flowers, its water source was naturally cut-off also. So, the flower wilted. And on the other hand, the flower that had the stem remained fresh for a much longer period of time.

Floating lemon

The fact

To determine whether a lemon will float in water or sink to the bottom.

What you need

- Whole lemon
- Bowl
- Water
- Knife
- Cutting board

How to do the experiment?

1. Fill the bowl with water in such a manner so that its about 3/4 full.
2. Place the whole lemon into the water. It floats!
3. Now cut the lemon into 4 pieces.
4. Place all the lemon pieces individually into the water. What happens?

What will happen?

The lemon sinks once it has been cut into 4 pieces.

A step further

You could try this experiment with other fruits as well. Can you think of a fruit that would always sink, regardless of being cut or not?

Conclusion

When the lemon pieces are put into the water they sink! This is because the lemon pulp gets filled with water after being cut. The weight of the water causes the lemon pieces to sink to the bottom of the bowl. The outer skin of the lemon is waterproof. And so, when not cut, due to this waterproof skin the lemon doesn't sink.

Taste and smell go together

The fact

We all know that some foods taste better than others. But have you ever thought what gives us the ability to experience all these unique flavours and tastes? This simple experiment shows that there's a lot more to taste than you might have thought before.

What you need

- A small piece of peeled potato
- A small piece of peeled apple

Note: both the fruits should be of the same shape so that you won't be able to tell the difference.

How to do the activity?

1. Close your eyes and mix up the pieces of potato and apple.
2. Hold your nose and eat each piece. What will happen? Can you tell the difference between the two fruits?

What will happen?

It will be difficult to tell the difference between the two fruits as you were holding your nose.

Conclusion

Our nose and mouth are connected through the same airway which means that you taste and smell foods at the same time. Your sense of taste can recognize salty, sweet, bitter and sour food; but when you combine this with your sense of smell you can recognize many other individual tastes as well.

Sunlight and plants

The fact

We all know that plants need sunlight in order to survive. This experiment will prove this.

What you need

- 2 plastic cups
- 2 saucers
- 2 seedlings
- soil
- water
- scissors

How to do the experiment?

1. Make some small holes in the bottom of the cups. This will help in draining out extra water from the cups.
2. Fill each cup with soil.
3. Plant a seedling in each cup in the centre of the soil and then cover it with soil again.
4. Place each cup on a saucer and pour equal amounts of water in both the cups.
5. Place one plant in a brightly lit room where it will get plenty of natural sunlight such as on a window sill.
6. Place the other plant in a dark area, devoid of natural light. Such locations include closets and drawers where doors can be shut and light kept out.
7. Leave both plants undisturbed for 3 or more days.
8. After several days have passed, observe your plants.

What will happen?

The plant that was placed in the dark room with no sunlight becomes limp and unhealthy, possibly even dead after only a few days. On the other hand, the plant which was kept in the sunlight, survived well.

Conclusion

Plants need natural sunlight to survive. They can be happy, healthy and growing only if they get the adequate amount of sunlight. This is because sunlight helps the plants to produce food, allowing them to stay healthy.

How yeast breathes

The fact

Most microorganisms are harmful to human beings as they cause various diseases. But some can also be very useful. We use them to make yoghurt, cheese, bread and beer. Yeast is a microscopic fungus which when dried looks like a yellowish powder. When observed under the microscope, it is found to consist of live cells. The given experiment shows how the yeast breathes.

How to do the experiment?

1. Put a teaspoonful of sugar and a small quantity of yeast into the bottle.
2. Add a little warm water. Shake to mix the ingredients.
3. Fix a balloon firmly over the neck of the bottle.
4. Pour warm water into the large vessel and put the bottle into it.

What will happen?

The balloon will blow up after sometime.

What you need

- A bottle
- Some sugar
- Dried yeast
- A large water vessel
- A balloon

Conclusion

After you have poured the warm water onto the yeast, it 'wakes up' and begins feeding on the sugar. As it does, it releases carbon dioxide during respiration and blows up the balloon with that gas.

Make your own greenhouse

What are we doing?

Creating a miniature greenhouse to grow living plants.

What is a greenhouse?

Greenhouses are structures made with glass or plastic and are mostly used to grow vegetables, fruits, plants, flowers and tobacco. Greenhouses protect plants from extreme cold along with storms and harsh weather. They also protect the plants from damaging pests.

What you need

- A clear plastic bottle (such as a large empty soda bottle)
- Planting soil
- Small plant or seedling
- Wide tape
- Scissors
- Water

How to do the activity?

1. Wash the bottle thoroughly so that it is clean. It is okay even if its still a little wet inside.
2. Cut the bottle into half.
3. Take the bottom part of the bottle and fill it half with soil.
4. Plant the seedling or small plant in the soil making sure to cover all its roots.
5. Place the top half of the bottle back onto the bottom half and seal them together with the tape. Make sure its air tight.
6. Put a few drops of water into the bottle. Replace the cap.
7. Place your mini greenhouse near a window where it will get plenty of sunlight. Leave it there for several days.
8. After a few days you will notice that the bottle has droplets of water. If the bottle becomes too moist, open the cap and let it dry for a while.

What happened?

The sun caused the temperature inside the greenhouse to rise. As the lid was sealed the air inside got heated, even when the air outside the greenhouse was cool. Moreover, the plant inside gave out water vapour as all plants do. The water vapour came in contact with the cool surface of the bottle and condensed to form tiny droplets of water.

Cells of an onion

The fact

An onion is made of many concentric layers. Each layer is separated by a thin membrane. In this experiment, we will make a slide and look at the cells of the membrane under a microscope.

What you need

- A small piece of onion
- Forceps or tweezers
- A clean glass slide
- Dye (iodine or methylene blue)
- Thin glass coverslip
- An optical microscope

How to do the experiment?

1. Take a small piece of onion and using forceps (tweezers) peel off the membrane from beneath.

2. Lay the membrane flat on the surface of a clean glass slide then add 1 drop of dye (iodine or methylene blue).

3. Lower a thin glass cover slip over the slide. Make sure there are no air bubbles.

4. Put the slide under the microscope. Make sure that the lens is set on low power, and the light of the microscope is turned on.

5. Look through the lens carefully until you see the cells. They will look like lizard skin.

6. Now use the high powered lens so that you can see the cells magnified. You should be able to make out the nucleus too.

How much air can your lungs hold?

The fact

Do you think you're fit and healthy? Let's check how much air your lungs can hold.

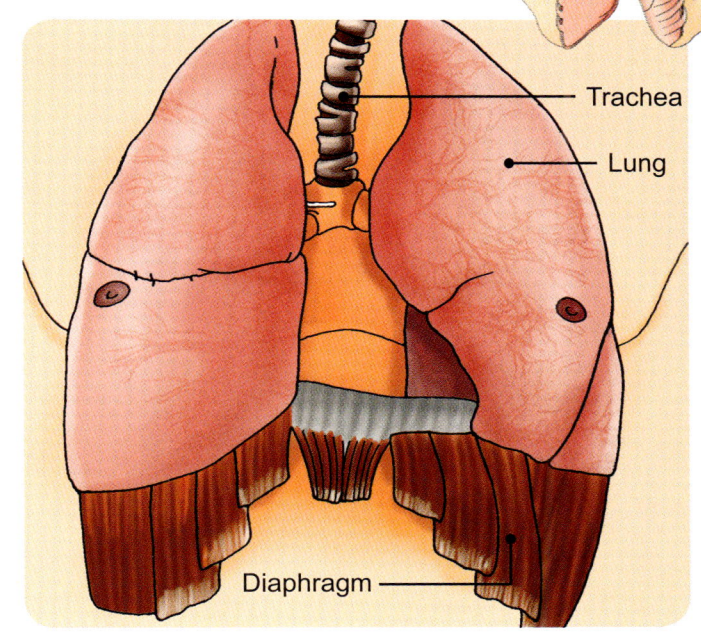

What you need

- Clean plastic tube
- A large plastic bottle
- Water
- Kitchen sink or large water basin

How to do the experiment?

1. Clean the plastic tube.
2. Put about 10 cm of water into your kitchen sink.
3. Fill the plastic bottle right to the top with water.
4. Put your hand over the top of the bottle to stop water from escaping when you turn it upside down.
5. Turn the bottle upside down. Place the top of the bottle under the water into the sink before removing your hand.
6. Push one end of the plastic tube into the bottle.
7. Take a big breath in.
8. Breathe out as much air as you can through the tube.

What will happen?

As you breathe out through the tube, the air from your lungs take the place of the water in the bottle. If you took a big breath in and breathed out fully then the volume of water you pushed out will be equivalent to how much air your lungs can hold.

Index

A
amoebas 23
arches 4

B
blind spot 19

C
capillary 6
concave 23
cuticle 5

D
dynamometer 16

E
Euglenas 23
eukaryotic 23

F
fungus 22, 28

G
geotropism 9
germinate 22

H
humus 14
hydrodynamics 11

M
macula 8

magnified 30
methylene blue 30
microorganisms 23

N
nucleus 30

O
osmotic pressure 6

P
potential energy 11
pressure 6, 11, 15, 18
Protozoa 23

R
resistance 20

S
stomata 13

T
transpiration 5, 13

U
unicellular 23

Y
Yellow Spot 8, 19